SPORTS ILLUSTRATED
BOOK OF DOG TRAINING

SPORTS ILLUSTRATED

Book of
DOG
TRAINING

BY THE EDITORS OF
SPORTS ILLUSTRATED

J. B. LIPPINCOTT COMPANY
Philadelphia and New York
1960

CONTENTS

1

THE FAMILY DOG

One of the most delightful—and perplexing—of all family problems begins when you bring home a new puppy. What happens from that moment on is up to you—his arrival can mean chaos and confusion, disrupted schedules and distraught tempers, or it can mean pleasure and companionship for every member of the family. Here Lois and Harland Meistrell of Great Neck, N.Y., who have worked with all breeds of dogs in their 25 years as both amateur and professional trainers, tell you how you can train your new puppy to be a rewarding and well-behaved addition to the family group.

INITIAL ADJUSTMENTS

A puppy, like a baby, is a bewildered creature in a strange world. Until he feels secure in his new environment he will either fear or fight it. First he needs a place of his own—and this should *not* be a lonely cellar or garage. Put him in a wire cage. Lined with a towel, it will double as a bed. In a cage like this he can see, be seen and be near you without getting underfoot. Speak to him whenever possible. He won't understand what you say but he will understand the tones you use. For the first week move his cage into your bedroom at night. Then he will know you are safely nearby and instead of whining he will sleep.

The easiest way to housebreak a puppy is to combine this training with exercise. Rig hardware-store wire into a playpen. Put newspaper in one corner and leave the pup here about 15 minutes every two hours. If he chooses the floor instead (he undoubtedly will the first few times), move the paper over the spot. Until he learns to associate paper with purpose, the only reprimand should be *no*. This is the first word he will have to learn; like all commands that follow, it should be short, simple and direct. Use the same pen in the transition from indoor to outdoor training. Before and after each meal put the pup outside in the pen. Since each change in routine means something new for him to learn, put a soiled newspaper in the pen with him. If you can't set the pen up outside, take along the paper anyway. It will help the puppy to understand what you expect of him—and don't expect too much. Few dogs are completely housebroken until about 6 months of age.

Wire cage doubles as bed and carrying case; permits pup to see, be seen and to adjust to surroundings.

Housebreaking pen can be set up in the kitchen or yard. Put newspaper in pen with pup. If he fails to use paper at first, reprimand him with stern *no* until association is established.

The proper way to
hold a new pup.

New puppies are most likely to be hurt, physically and
psychologically, by overeager children. Immature dogs are
fragile—their bones break easily and internal injuries often
result from good-natured roughhousing. If you have a young
child and a new pup, each must learn to respect as well as
enjoy the other. Begin by teaching your child to pick up
pup with one hand supporting his chest and the other his
hindquarters. In this way the pup cannot squirm out of the
child's grip or twist into a harmful position. Remind the
child to talk to the puppy, so he will be at ease. In play,
discourage quick lunges at the dog. Any movement from
behind—especially rapid movement—frightens a puppy, because he doesn't see or understand it. Let the child bring
himself down to the dog's level by sitting on the floor and
waiting—sooner or later natural curiosity will attract pup to
child. In this way the dog will learn to expect comfort and
approval rather than harm from his young owner.

4

To pick up pup correctly, put hands under dog's chest and hindquarters, distributing the puppy's weight and preventing him from falling.

Playing with pup can be harmful and frightening when child lunges at dog (*left*). Wait for pup on his level, permit him to approach voluntarily.

Training to the lead should begin early. The new pup first learns to wear leather collar, then to walk on a loose lead.

TRAINING TO THE LEAD

From the moment a new puppy enters the home, he should learn to wear a small leather collar. One with bells will help you keep track of his whereabouts. As soon as he becomes used to it (this will take two or three days), attach a light lead and let him drag it about. This helps reduce any wildness or fear many young pups show when first on a lead. After a few days pick up one end of the lead and hold it loosely while you walk around the yard or home. Don't try to pull or direct the dog; all you want to do now is to acquaint him with this limited check on his freedom. The secret here, as in all training, is to remember to talk to him. At first he may be confused about his role. If he strains at the lead or chews on it, correct him by saying *no*. If he persists, accompany *no* with a quick jerk on the lead. As soon as he understands what you expect, he'll try to comply, because dogs,

6

Pressing down on hindquarters to make the dog sit from standing position is shown by trainer, who accompanies action with command *sit*. Pup should be on loose lead.

Pulling up by loose neck skin is harmless way to raise a lazy puppy to the correct sit position. Remember to give command *sit* at same time.

LEARNING TO SIT

like children, basically want to please you. When he is good, let him know by scratching his ears and praising him.

Next your dog must learn to sit at your command. Again, this is a puppy exercise, so have patience with him. Stand stationary, holding the lead in one hand. As you say *sit*, press down on his hindquarters with the other. If the dog lies down instead, grasp the loose skin at his neck as shown above and pull up until he is sitting (this won't hurt him). Repeat the command *sit*. Since you have now added another word to his vocabulary, don't confuse the puppy by varying the command—and don't weaken it by also using his name. Praise him as soon as he sits. By the time your pup is 3 months old, he should have mastered this exercise. Now he will be ready to learn the more advanced lessons that follow.

7

FIRST FORMAL TRAINING

SIT-STAY COMMAND

Preliminary

The most important exercise you can teach your dog is to sit and stay on command. Once he learns this, you can leave him anywhere and know he will be there when you return. Wait until he is at least 3 months old before beginning the sit-stay. Your puppy should now recognize his name, be familiar with the lead and respond to the simple command *sit*. Use a longer lead (six to eight feet) than normal so you and the dog can move freely. Holding the slack loosely in the right hand, walk the dog briefly, then bring him in as close to your left foot as possible. Give the command *sit*. As soon as he sits, reward him by stroking his head (don't pat—few dogs appreciate being thumped on the head). Now shift the lead to the other hand and swing forward in a half-circle so that you are facing the dog. Give the command *stay*. At the same time bring your right hand—fingers together, palm forward—to the dog's nose to block his moving ahead. Keep all motions smooth. If your pup drops his head, repeat *stay* and tap him lightly under his chin. Follow by again bringing your hand to his nose. Avoid excessive correction by anticipating your dog's errors and rewarding him *before* he has time to commit them. In this way he will associate pleasure with doing what you want. Repeat several times, then let pup romp briefly before undertaking the remainder of exercise.

8

Preliminary sit-stay begins with dog in sit position. The trainer faces dog, holding lead in the left hand. On the command *stay*, he brings palm to dog's nose, preventing any break from sit position.

Intermediate stage begins with dog in
the initial sit-stay position. Holding
the lead loosely above dog's head for
minimum control, trainer walks slowly
in a circle, repeating the command
stay whenever necessary.

Final stage introduces the dog to working off lead. On *stay*, trainer walks away, reinforcing command by moving arm toward dog to stop him from breaking or following.

Intermediate

Once your dog has mastered the preliminaries, he must learn to remain in the stay position even when you are not present. Repeat the initial exercise. Then, with lead in your left hand, straighten to a standing position and walk slowly around the dog. If he stands too, start again. Help him along by repeating the command *stay*, and be careful not to confuse him by jerking or pulling on the lead.

Final

Now drop the lead and go through the exercise exactly as before. As you move around the dog, increase each circle until you are about 10 feet away from him. After a rest, again run through the initial sit-stay, only this time, instead of walking around the dog, turn away from him and walk about five feet. Watch him over your shoulder, saying *stay* when necessary. With each successive run-through increase the distance between you and the dog until you can actually leave the room without his moving. It will take at least four training sessions and a maximum of patience to teach your dog this exercise. But once he has learned it, you will be able to leave him alone, in a parked car, in somebody else's home—or anywhere—with the confidence that he will stay on your command.

Walking briskly to sustain the dog's interest, trainer holds lead loosely in his right hand, keeps left hand on lead near collar to help guide dog as he vocally encourages him to *heel*.

WALKING AT HEEL

Taking your dog for a walk should be fun for you and for him. It certainly won't be if he pulls and fights on the lead, or—if he is a big dog—literally drags you behind him. Nor does he have to be a show dog to learn to walk at heel obediently in about three lessons. Begin with the dog in a sit position on your left. With the end of the lead in your right hand, put your left hand close to his collar to direct him. On the command *heel*, walk forward. A fast pace will keep the dog alert and his attention from wandering. When you stop, say *sit* immediately and follow with praise. Once your dog learns this much, he will no longer need the guidance of your hand near his collar. If you have a large breed, such as the Rhodesian ridgeback being trained here, use a chain choke-collar during training to prevent his breaking away from you. Keep dog close to your left side as you walk. Always maintain a firm grip with both hands on the lead but do not hold it taut. Should the dog lunge forward, one short jerk on the lead is much more effective than a long, weak pull. If he continues to pull, stop, bring the lead up short, and say *no*. Enforce this correction when necessary by slapping across the forequarters with the end of the lead. Never let any dog, especially a big dog, intimidate or take advantage of you. And always remember that tone of voice in correction is more important than volume. Your dog will be happier, and so will you, when he learns to obey your commands.

Jerking sharply on the lead (*above*) when dog breaks, trainer shows the best hand position for maximum control during advanced stage of exercise, and relaxed lead on choke-collar.

Rewarding dog at the end of the *heel* exercise, trainer brings him to sit position close to left leg, strokes dog's head to show approval.

Persuading dog to stay when down, the trainer combines hand movement with command *stay*, keeps all movements slow, voice gentle to avoid exciting or confusing the dog.

Helping dog to stay when standing, trainer holds hand against inside leg joint and, when necessary, pulls dog up by lead.

DOWN AND STAND-STAY

Your dog now knows how to sit and stay on command. Teaching him to stay when lying down or standing follows naturally. To make him lie down, begin in the sit position. On the command *down,* press on his shoulders with one hand as you motion him down with the other. Face him when you do this, so he knows you are not going to hurt him. If he remains sitting, repeat the command *down* as you pull his forelegs towards you. This will make him lie down. As soon as he does, give the command *stay*. Praise him immediately. To teach your dog to stay when standing, walk him on a loose lead, then stop and give the command *stand,* followed by *stay*. Prevent him from sitting by putting your hand against the joint of his hind leg as shown above. You may have to help him by looping the lead under his hindquarters and pulling upward as you give the commands.

15

Leather collar is adequate for a thoroughly obedient dog at this stage of training.

COME COMMAND

The most neglected training exercise is teaching your dog to come when you call him. The frustration of trying to get your dog's attention by shouting, whistling and rapping a spoon on his bowl can be avoided if you teach him the command *come* as soon as he completes his basic training. Put your dog in the sit-stay position. With a long lead held loosely in one hand, walk a few feet away and face him, bending slightly forward. If your dog is small, instead of bending forward, squat down so you are closer to his level. Any variation on a training method which helps your dog to understand better what you expect of him makes the exercise more enjoyable. On the command *come,* jerk sharply on the lead. When he comes to you, stroke his head and praise him. Each time you run through the exercise, increase the distance you walk from the dog. Then, drop the lead and repeat. If he tries to follow you or starts to break before your command, instead of reprimanding him, say *come* immediately. With a minimum of correction, he will learn faster and associate fun with the exercise.

Beginning exercise, trainer puts the dog in a basic sit-stay position. Holding lead loosely, she walks away, then faces dog and bends slightly toward him.

Following through, trainer jerks lead on command *come*. As soon as the dog obeys command and comes to trainer, he should be rewarded with praise.

17

PRACTICAL DISCIPLINE

CAR CHASING

Young puppies are inclined to chase anything that moves. As they grow older this tendency often turns to chasing cars. Your dog won't understand that a car means danger unless you teach him. If he has never chased a car, the best way to insure that he never will is to make him afraid of all cars. Fear, like praise, has a specific role in training. For this lesson you need a piece of split bamboo, which combines a loud, cracking noise with a harmless but stinging blow when you strike the dog. Holding lead firmly in one hand, walk your dog up to a car. When he is close to it, strike first the fender of the car and then dog's chest with the bamboo. Make this a single motion from car to dog. At the same time say *no* and jerk sharply on the lead. If your dog is a confirmed car chaser, you can try this method, too; but you will probably find more severe measures are necessary. The method recommended here can be dangerous, so put two collars and two leads on your dog to prevent his breaking free. You will also need two assistants—one to drive a car and the other to sit in the back seat armed with several tin cans filled with pebbles. Take a firm grip on both leads close to the collars as shown left. When the car drives by, let your dog begin to chase it. Then, on the command *no,* jerk sharply on the leads. At the same time have your assistant throw one or more of the tin cans at the dog. You may have to repeat this lesson several times, but it is one your dog must learn. Until he does, no training measure is too severe when weighed against the injuries which sooner or later befall car chasers.

18

Preventing car chasing by deliberately instilling fear of autos, trainer walks the dog on a lead close to a car, strikes fender, then dog with bamboo on command *no*.

Correcting car chaser is dangerous training. Two collars and leads are essential to prevent dog's breaking free.

19

Training aid of split bamboo is useful in all discipline, as it combines a loud noise with a stinging but harmless blow. Basis of corrective training is developing in your dog an association between unpleasant experience and forbidden object.

MANNERS

The easiest way to insure good manners in your dog is to prevent his developing bad ones. Few dogs disobey deliberately; generally they don't know they are doing wrong, and won't know until you show them. When your dog first jumps on furniture or people, say *no* immediately. If he continues, walk him to the furniture and strike it and then the dog as you command *no*. When your dog jumps on you, rap him on the nose or head with three fingers as you reprimand him. With a big dog, on *no* bring your knee to his chest in one sharp blow. Don't be angry; remember that basically he wants to please you. When he does, praise him so he knows.

All puppies like to chew things, and some have expensive tastes. Give your pup something of his own to chew on. When he chooses something of yours instead, reprimand him. If he still refuses to give up the object, put your hand, as shown, over his muzzle with forefinger and thumb just above his lip so they exert pressure on his canine teeth. This way he will not be able to bite you and will be forced to let you take the object from his mouth. Say *give* in a stern tone. It's not necessary to break a dog's spirit to make him behave. If you show him what you want of him, correct him as soon as he does wrong and reward him when he obeys you, all of his habits can be good ones.

20

Jumping on furniture is corrected (*above*) by the method used to prevent car chasing. When reprimand fails, trainer hits furniture, then dog with split bamboo on command *no*.

Chewing your things is common in young pups, rarely deliberate. If dog refuses to drop object on command *no*, put hand over muzzle so forefinger and thumb exert pressure on his canine teeth, enabling you to remove object from mouth.

ADVANCED FORMAL TRAINING

HEEL OFF LEAD

The most challenging test of your dog's obedience to your commands comes when you introduce him to walking without a lead. Work alone in an enclosed area so your dog won't be distracted or run away. Romp with him briefly; then, on lead, review his past lessons to make sure he knows them perfectly. With your dog in sit position, take the lead around your back and hold it in your right hand as shown below. Give the command *heel*. Remember to walk briskly to keep his attention. Until now your dog has been used to being controlled by the lead so if he doesn't follow you the first few times, guide him by holding his collar. Next, hang the lead loosely over your left arm and repeat the exercise. At first your dog may not walk as close to you as you want, but

Stage One in teaching your dog to heel off lead begins with lead passed behind trainer, held loosely in his right hand. Left hand is used for initial guidance.

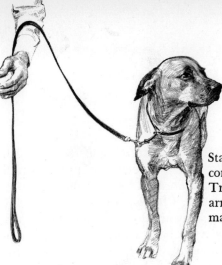

Stage Two further reduces control of the lead over dog. Trainer loops lead over his arm, directs dog by vocal command only.

Stage Three simulates off-lead work as the trainer drapes the lead over his shoulder for minimum control. Obedience is more important here than precision.

right now obedience is more important than precision. The object is to make him heel with minimum guidance from the lead. When he does, praise him. Then reduce the lead control even more by draping it over your right shoulder. Repeat the exercise. Your dog should now be ready to walk off lead. Keep the detached lead in your hand. If he breaks, correct him immediately by slapping him on the rump. Always begin in the sit position, and make the command *heel* forceful. This new freedom may confuse your dog at first, so be patient and praise him liberally when he obeys. Once he learns this lesson, you will be proud to take him anywhere.

SIMPLE TRICKS

Beg

All dogs enjoy showing-off. You can enjoy it too, by teaching yours a few tricks. To make him beg, begin in a sit position. On the command *beg*, raise him by the front legs so he sits up. With the other hand, lift his chin as shown below and repeat command *beg*. If your dog has trouble keeping his balance at first, support his back against a wall. Once he is sitting up, praise him liberally. This is a good time to introduce a small tidbit as reward.

Teaching to beg begins in sit position. On the command *beg*, trainer lifts dog's foot and chin, then steadies dog until he regains balance.

Roll Over

To make him roll over, put him in a down position. Pull his far foreleg toward you with one hand as you push his shoulder away from you with the other. At the same time, command *roll over*.

Teaching to roll over begins (*left*) with down position. On command *roll over*, trainer pulls dog's far foreleg toward him, at same time pushes his shoulder away.

Pray

You can teach him to pray by having him sit in front of a chair. On the command *pray,* lift his forefeet up so they rest on the edge of the chair, and press his head down gently on his paws. Here, as in all training, you must associate one clear, concise command with the lesson you want your dog to learn. And he will enjoy learning new lessons if his reward is immediate and enthusiastic praise.

Fetch

Teaching to fetch is useful exercise which can be combined with breaking dog of chewing your things. Open dog's mouth as previously shown. On command *fetch,* put a rolled piece of paper between his teeth (*above, right*). Remove your hand, reward the dog with praise. Then cup your hand and hold it in front of him as you command *give*. If he refuses, open his mouth until the paper drops into your hand, then reward. As soon as he understands what you want, hold the paper in front of him and command *fetch*. Repeat, moving the paper farther away. Now you are ready to teach him to retrieve.

25

RETRIEVING ON COMMAND

Once your dog becomes used to fetching a rolled paper, he can then learn to retrieve any object. You will appreciate this lesson when you drop something or want him to fetch your evening paper or slippers. Begin with the dog on lead for maximum control. At this stage you can substitute a glove or slipper for the rolled paper. With the dog in sit position, drop the object on the ground a few feet from him. Command *fetch*. Reinforce the command by pointing at the object if your dog seems confused. As soon as he picks it up,

26

Intermediate stage in retrieving is taught on lead. Trainer guides dog over a bench (*foreground*), then sends dog over bench alone on command *fetch*.

say *come*. When he returns to you, command *give,* then praise him so he knows you are pleased. Throw the object farther away from him each time. When he knows this stage thoroughly, turn a bench on its side as shown above and put the object on one side. Holding the lead loosely in your left hand, make the dog sit next to you on the other side of the bench. On the command *fetch,* walk briskly forward and over the bench. If the dog hesitates, direct him by pulling slightly on the lead. When he picks up the object, lead him back over the bench, command *sit,* then *give*. Next, send him over the bench alone.

From here, it is just a matter of practice to teach him to jump higher barriers. And you needn't worry about his jumping the fence when you're away if he has learned to act only on your command. In fact, if you train your dog to obey and respect you at all times, you will never have to worry about him at all.

Final stage finds dog willing to jump high fences to retrieve any object on command. If your dog has learned obedience, he will only jump when ordered.

2

THE FIELD DOG

Most hunters who have ever owned gun dogs agree that with few exceptions these dogs also make fine house pets. More surprising, perhaps, is the fact that many house pets make excellent gun dogs without losing any of the qualities which endear them to the family at home. In this section, four experts offer instructions in the training of field dogs. Photographs of the 22 most popular sporting breeds appear in Section 3.

Before receiving field training, each dog should, of course, learn the simple rules of living with people. When he has mastered the commands to sit, to stay, to come when called, he is ready to take to the field.

THE FLUSHING SPANIELS

Cocker and springer spaniels are especially adaptable to the dual role of hunting and home companions. American and English cocker spaniels and English and Welsh springer spaniels, in particular, are easy to teach, eager to learn and generally enthusiastic by nature. Given proper training, almost any spaniel can fulfill both roles and add immeasurably to his master's enjoyment. For most spaniels, the right age will be between six and nine months. Up to a year and a half, the average dog.can still be taught to hunt, but much beyond this age training may be more difficult.

The flushing spaniel is perhaps the most versatile of all the sporting breeds, performing a triple job in the field. Not only will he find game, he will also flush it to the gun and retrieve it. The flushing spaniel seeks his game close to the hunter and within shotgun range. This characteristic, combined with a natural retrieving instinct, makes him a special favorite of the pheasant and grouse shooter who likes to hunt his birds on foot and at a reasonable pace.

THE TRAILING HOUNDS

Bloodhound, basset hound, beagle, black and tan coonhound and dachshund are the most popular trailing hounds in America today; but in addition to these dogs, countless mixed strains are used for tracking. Most often, they follow rabbits, but these plodding and determined trackers also trail raccoons, foxes, deer and sometimes even people. Regardless of quarry, all of the trailing hounds share one trait— an extraordinary ability to follow a ground trail by scent. They must be taught, nonetheless, to concentrate their superior ability on a single scent and to follow it without interruption, no matter what other scents may cross the trail. This is the basis of all hound training, whether the dog be a basset after a rabbit or a bloodhound helping rescue a lost child.

The amenable, relaxed, almost lazy disposition of the hound has made him so adaptable as a family pet that in recent years he has spent more time indoors and less in the field. Yet the qualities which made him such a good pet are combined with a superior nose and surprising physical endurance, qualifying the hound as a steadfast hunting expert. The desire to hunt is a powerful instinct in all hounds, and even the most sluggish family dog can become a good trailer.

THE RUGGED RETRIEVERS

The most rugged of all the sporting dogs, retrievers are specially equipped, both physically and temperamentally, for their strenuous job. In this country, the most popular are Chesapeake Bay, curly-coated, golden and Labrador retrievers, Irish water spaniel and poodle. All of these breeds are built for rough work in the outdoors, and specifically for use in duck and goose shooting.

Once a bird has been downed, the retriever is expected to locate it, regardless of where it has fallen, and deliver it to the hunter. Fine eyesight and a steady, determined disposition help the retriever do his job; but his most important features are his dense waterproof coat, heavy muscular structure and superb swimming ability, which enable him to work under the most adverse outdoor conditions. In fact, many retrievers actually seem to be at their best in freezing temperatures, icy winds, and storm-tossed seas. For duck and goose hunters, especially northern hunters who shoot over water, retrievers can be excellent hunting companions, and, equally important, they can contribute a great deal to conservation by preventing the waste of crippled and lost birds.

31

THE POINTING DOGS

The desire to point is instinctive and exists to a limited degree in all dogs. In the pointing breeds, however, it has been specifically developed and intensified over the years. These dogs have further been bred for speed and physical stamina to enable them to hunt quickly and skillfully over vast areas of game cover. While the Brittany spaniel, Weimaraner and German shorthair are relative newcomers to the American hunting scene, the Irish, Gordon and English setters are oldtime favorites now making a comeback in the field after years of over-breeding for show. They have the same natural instinct for finding birds as the pointer, who has dominated quail shooting for decades.

The pointing dog's job is to work out ahead of the hunter and when he smells game literally to point it out to the man who follows him. One of the most dramatic experiences for a hunter in the field is the sight of a dog on point, his body tense and rigid, his nose extended in the direction of game. Once the pointing dog is frozen in this attitude, he will remain for a minute or an hour, if need be, while the hunter moves up to flush the bird. For the upland bird shooter, particularly the quail hunter, whether he seeks his game on horseback or on foot, a pointing dog is certainly his most valuable companion.

In training any breed of field dog, the by-words for the trainer are *practice* and *patience*. Flushing spaniels, trailing hounds, rugged retrievers and pointing dogs must be carefully trained before they can be expected to do a good job in the field. It is important to remember that dogs, like people, are individuals; some learn more quickly than others.

With practice and patience, training can be for the hunter, as well as the dog, a rewarding and exciting experience. Moreover, trainers frequently find that a dog becomes a better companion at home when he has learned to be a companion afield.

THE FLUSHING SPANIELS

Stanley MacQueen

Stanley MacQueen is the third generation of MacQueens to take up gun-dog training and has spent the major part of his 30 years working with flushing spaniels. This interest began in childhood under the guidance of his famous father, the international spaniel authority Larry MacQueen. Now father and son together train and handle more than 100 spaniels every year at their Ramornie Kennels in Pottersville, N.J. In the ultimate test of gun-dog training, the MacQueens have been represented at every national spaniel field-trial run in this country, and they have won national championships three times.

Training pistol accustoms
pup to gunfire in the field.

Short runs acquaint puppy
with thickets and brush.

Shallow pond for splashing
introduces young dog to water.

FIRST TIME IN THE FIELD

The opening phase of field training is easy and very informal. It involves no more than taking the young dog out in the field as often as possible to acquaint him with all types of terrain and game cover. A spaniel is born with a natural desire to hunt. Your job is to encourage this birdiness, as it is called, by making his outdoor sessions fun. Keep them short—a half hour every day rather than several consecutive hours once a week—and stop them, for a few days if necessary, when the dog seems to be tired or losing interest. The basic equipment you will need is a collar and lead, a whistle (police variety), and a .22-caliber blank training pistol. Always take the dog afield on the lead, and before releasing him make him sit, so he understands you are the boss. Let him run free for a few minutes while he works off excess energy, then walk along in the direction he takes. When he gets too far ahead of you, call him back. Each time you call him, follow the command with several short whistle blasts. Eventually he will learn to associate this whistle signal with the voice command "Come." If he is slow at first, be patient, and avoid excessive correction. It is more important now that he develop interest in a variety of cover than that he obeys every command. If he is reluctant to enter heavy brush or briers, encourage him by going in first. When you come to water, let him splash and play in it. After the dog has been afield several times, accustom him to the sound of gunfire by shooting the training pistol in the air. Make sure he is at least 100 yards away from you the first few times you fire so that you don't startle him. Gradually decrease the distance as he becomes used to the noise. When you are ready to leave the field for home, reward the pup with stroking and praise as you put him back on the lead. Remember that the most important part of this early training is to make it fun for the dog. It will be if every session afield is relaxed and short.

35

Praise is the best reward
at end of session afield.

FIRST ENCOUNTER WITH BIRDS

As soon as the pup is ranging freely, sniffing eagerly for
signs of game, and entering all kinds of cover with boldness,
he is ready for his first encounter with birds. At this stage
is is not important that they be pheasants or grouse; pigeons
are cheaper and easier to handle. Clip the flight feathers
from one wing to prevent the bird from flying. Hold the
pigeon in your hand, and let the dog sniff and nuzzle it. Then
shake it slightly—this won't hurt the bird but will dizzy it

so it stays in one spot—and throw it a few feet from you. Encourage the dog to go after the pigeon by moving your arm toward it and saying "Fetch." He will probably pick it up right away but he may decide to play with it. It is better to let him do so briefly the first few times than risk souring him on birds by correcting him. As soon as he takes the bird in his mouth whistle him to you. If he returns without the bird, repeat "Fetch" and encourage him by whistle and voice to bring it. When he does, reward him. Repeat this exercise daily, planting the bird farther away each time. And remember, be patient with his mistakes and generous with praise.

Let puppy sniff the bird to acquaint him with game scent.

Encourage dog to find bird and bring it back to you.

BEGINNING CONTROLS

After the dog has some field experience behind him and is used to retrieving live birds, he is ready for the basic exercises which will control him when hunting. Hand and whistle commands are the tools with which you exercise control. The whistle is actually a substitute for the voice commands he has learned at home; in the field it is more valuable than the voice because it carries farther and with more authority. The dog already knows that a series of short blasts means "Come." The next and more formal whistle command is the

sit-stay. Begin with the voice command "Sit-stay." Follow it immediately with a single, sharp whistle blast, and reinforce it by holding your hand, palm toward the dog, as shown at left. Then move slowly away, steadying him with your hand and repeating the single whistle blast if he tries to follow you. Once he masters this command—and it may require weeks of training—he will stop and sit to the whistle whenever he hears it.

Control begins with single whistle blast meaning *"Sit."*

Command is reinforced by hand and voice signals.

FIELD DIRECTIONS

A flushing dog must stay within range of the gun (not more than 40 to 50 yards from you) and hunt all cover around you. On the previous page you learned how to stop him by whistle anywhere in the field. The next step is to send, or cast, him off to hunt in another direction. Begin with the dog in sit position. Send him to the left or right by moving your arm and body in that direction. Accompany the arm signal with two short whistle blasts. The double whistle blast is used to send the dog in any direction; the arm signal indicates the direction he is to go. As the dog ranges ahead of you, whistle him to stop. Then, with your arm and whistle, cast him in a new direction. Repeat the signals daily until he understands them. When he does, you will be able to control the distance he ranges and the area he hunts.

Arm signals direct puppy; whistle sends him to hunt.

Trainer casts dog to the right with arm motion.

Outward movement of
hand sends dog ahead.

FLUSHED BIRDS

When you have acquired control of the way your dog ranges
in the field—this takes two to three months of daily training—
he is ready for the final exercise before an actual hunt: re-
sponse to a flushed bird. This is called steadying the dog to
wing and shot. Use a scented dummy instead of a bird for
this training. At first, the dog will be easier to handle on a
check rope. Holding the rope loosely, whistle the dog to sit.
Throw the dummy in front of him and fire the training
pistol. If he starts after the dummy, repeat the single whistle
blast and pull sharply on the rope. The dog should remain

Check rope is looped loosely
at dog's neck, and prevents
him from breaking.

steady until you give the signal to retrieve. Repeat the exercise, gradually moving farther away from the dog. Each time, throw the dummy closer to him. This will tempt the spaniel to break. If he does, correct him immediately. Remove the rope only when he is steady. This is one of the difficult exercises to teach, but when the dog learns it, he is ready to go hunting.

Throw dummy close to dog
to simulate a flushed bird.

The dog must retrieve
only upon command.

THE HUNT

The most fun and the most interesting part of training a spaniel for the field begins when you take him out after live game. It can also be a trying time for the novice trainer because his dog must face a number of new experiences. This will be the young spaniel's first encounter with birds that fly, with the louder noise of a shotgun instead of a training pistol, and with having birds shot over him. You can make it easier for the dog, and give yourself more freedom to control him, if you take along a friend to do the shooting. A .410 shotgun on the first few hunts will also be less startling than a bigger, noisier gun like a 12-gauge. Pigeons are still the least expensive birds to use during these first shooting sessions. Before taking the dog into the field, dizzy several pigeons and plant them at intervals in the cover. Then with your friend walking slightly apart and abreast of you, start the dog hunting. You will have greater control over him if you limit his range to a maximum of 30 yards at first. Be on the alert at all

Teaching control is easier if a friend does shooting.

Dog should sit or "hup"
as soon as bird flushes.

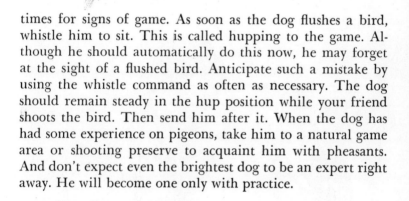

times for signs of game. As soon as the dog flushes a bird,
whistle him to sit. This is called hupping to the game. Although he should automatically do this now, he may forget
at the sight of a flushed bird. Anticipate such a mistake by
using the whistle command as often as necessary. The dog
should remain steady in the hup position while your friend
shoots the bird. Then send him after it. When the dog has
had some experience on pigeons, take him to a natural game
area or shooting preserve to acquaint him with pheasants.
And don't expect even the brightest dog to be an expert right
away. He will become one only with practice.

Spaniel must remain steady
while hunter shoots the bird.

HIGH POINT

The reward of these training sessions afield and the high point of the hunt will come when your spaniel retrieves his first wild bird and brings it triumphantly to you. This is the climax of the months you have worked with him in the field, and it is also the moment when a sportsman realizes that, besides a pet, he owns a useful and intelligent gun dog. When you whistle him back after the bird has been downed, remember that the dog will expect and deserve some praise from you. Give it to him enthusiastically, because now he is a hunter and has earned it.

THE TRAILING HOUNDS

Fred Huyler

Ever since Fred Huyler was given a beagle as a pet in 1886, hounds and hunting have been his career. As a young man he was hired to train hounds at Hamilton Farms in Gladstone, N.J. Since then, the number of dogs he has trained and field trials he has run cannot be counted. In the following pages, Huyler shares the lessons of 70 years afield in teaching you how to train trailing hounds for the chase.

BLOODHOUNDS

Teaching a bloodhound to follow a trail is informal, fun and the foundation of most trailing-hound training. Since a bloodhound is almost always used to track people, you will need the cooperation of a friend. You will also need a harness and a sturdy lead, both of which are necessary for all future tracking. To begin the training, have your friend walk off a short, easy trail, ending behind a· bush or tree. Make it about 150 yards for a starter, and agree in advance on its course. When your friend is out of sight, let the dog sniff an item of his clothing—preferably a sock. Then have the dog sniff the place on the ground where the trail begins. When a bloodhound puts his nose to the ground, the loose folds of skin around his head sag forward, forming a cup to trap scent. If you pull the skin on his neck forward (*right*), you will help him get a better sniff. Once he associates the garment with the ground scent, his natural instinct will be to follow the trail. Encourage him with your voice. If the dog wanders from the trail or loses interest in it, let him sniff the clothing again. Keep a firm grip on the lead at all times and move at the dog's pace so he doesn't think you are pulling him back. When he comes to the end of the trail, the dog should leap up on his quarry to indicate he has found the person he was tracking. Most bloodhounds will do this naturally. If yours doesn't, encourage him by having your friend give him a tidbit as soon as the dog reaches him. Take the dog out as often as possible, each time increasing the length and difficulty of the trail. And be patient with his mistakes. The average bloodhound needs at least six months of regular training to follow a trail without error.

Bloodhound gets the scent by sniffing clothing of his quarry.

Trainer stays close behind as the dog takes off on the trail.

Hound associates scent of clothing with ground trail.

Hound follows the scent to hiding place behind bush.

Dog jumps up on quarry to show positive identification.

GAME HOUNDS

Like the bloodhound, the other trailing hounds—beagles, bassets, dachshunds and coonhounds—must learn to concentrate on a single track before they are ready to go on a real hunt. And since these other breeds are small game hunters, a game trail instead of a human trail is used in training them. For this early training, it will be much easier for both you and the dog if you make an artificial trail, which you do by saturating a bag of sawdust with commercial game scent and dragging it about 100 yards. Then, with the dog on lead, take him to the place where the trail starts. When he locates the scent, encourage him to follow it and correct him if he wanders. At the end of the trail, reward him with praise and a tidbit. When he has learned to follow an easy trail, remove the lead and drag the scent through brush and briers so he gets used to more difficult routes. Spend at least two months on this stage of training.

Take dog on lead to place where artificial trail begins.

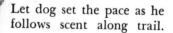

Let dog set the pace as he follows scent along trail.

FIRST ENCOUNTER WITH GAME

As soon as the dog can follow an artificial trail, he is ready for live game. At this stage the type of game—regardless of what the dog will eventually hunt—is not important as long as it leaves a simple, obvious trail. A rabbit from a pet shop is easy to care for and slow enough for a young dog to keep up with. This training should take place in an enclosed area so both the game and the dog are under control. Let the dog sniff the rabbit while a friend holds it. Then take the dog out of sight and release the rabbit. Unleash the dog and encourage him to find and follow the rabbit's trail. An older dog can help in this training by leading the way. In any case, stay close behind so you can separate dogs and rabbit if necessary. Take the dog out with the rabbit for about a week and keep the sessions short so the dog will not lose his enthusiasm.

Dog sniffs rabbit to become acquainted with the scent.

Rabbit is released and dog sets out on chase.

FIRST TIME IN THE FIELD

The most challenging phase of hound training occurs when you go afield after wild game. Now the trail may lead anywhere; it may be old or it may not exist at all. But the measure of a good trailing hound is experience, and the only way he will gain it is by hunting as often as possible. Again, an older dog can be of help during these sessions because the young dog will follow him and learn by imitation. Whether you take the dog afield alone or with another dog, however, always take him on lead so that he knows you are the boss.

On first hunt, bring an older dog along as guide for pup.

Try to keep close to dog and use light-gauge gun.

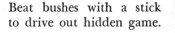

Beat bushes with a stick
to drive out hidden game.

When you reach the hunting area, release the dog and encourage him to start hunting by talking to him as you walk through the woods. Many people find the chase itself so enjoyable that they never shoot over their trailing hounds. Nevertheless, it is a good idea to acquaint your dog with gunfire so that he will not be frightened by it. You can do this by carrying along a shotgun (a .410 is better than a larger gauge at first because it makes less noise) and firing it from time to time when the dog is actually on a trail and at least 50 yards from you. In areas where game is scarce or cover is dense, beat the bushes with a stick as you walk along. Rabbits and other small game often sit tight at the approach of danger and can sometimes be routed out of hiding by such action. And always be on the alert for signs of game. You may see an animal take off before the dog is able to scent it. If you do, call him back to you and help him locate the trail.

Trainer shows dog place where game trail begins.

RUNNING A FRESH TRAIL

When you locate a fresh game trail, the pup will probably bound off on the scent, particularly if there is an older dog along. If he does not, start him on the trail by pointing out the way. You will know he is on scent when you hear the deep-throated baying that all game hounds instinctively sound when they hit a fresh track. This is the climax of the chase and the reward for the many hours of training. For whether you hunt with a gun or for the chase alone, the musical cry of a tracker closing in on his quarry is one of the most exciting sounds in the field.

Young dog takes lead from older dog in following trail.

Dogs leave the field on lead at end of day's hunt.

THE RUGGED RETRIEVERS

James A. Cowie

Son of a Scottish gamekeeper, James Cowie of Commack, N.Y. grew up handling gun dogs in Pitlochry, Scotland. Since coming to this country in 1920 he has schooled hundreds of retrievers, and three times in succession won the Labrador Retriever Club Championship.

EARLY FIELD TRAINING

A retriever is born with an instinct to fetch, and he usually shows signs of it by playfully picking up any object thrown to him. This does not mean that he is ready to start his formal field training. You may actually discourage his natural instincts if you try to train him too early. Most dogs are not ready until they are about 9 months old. Some Labradors can be started sooner, but Chesapeakes and goldens often do better when training begins at 11 or 12 months. Until this time take the pup out every day (or as often as possible) for runs of no more than 15 minutes and just introduce him to the outdoors. Walk with him through fields and brush so he gets used to varied terrain. Let him play with a glove by throwing it to him. When he picks it up, call him back to you by blowing several short, soft blasts on a training whistle. Praise him if he fetches it to you but don't correct him if he does not. Your goal now is simply to acquaint him with the outdoors and with one simple whistle command.

Blow whistle to call pup
to you as he retrieves glove.

Hold dog in sit position, then throw training dummy.

FORMAL EXERCISES

When the pup is used to the outdoors and has learned the basic sit, stay, and come commands from his home training, he is ready to start formal work in the field. Begin by making him sit. Take hold of his collar and throw a training dummy about 10 yards. Release him on the command, "Fetch," and direct him toward the dummy with a sweeping movement of your arm. As soon as he picks up the dummy, whistle him back to you. If he runs the other way, don't chase after him. Instead step back and call him by name. When he finally comes to you, be ready to take the dummy from him before he drops it. Spend several weeks on this exercise and ignore his mistakes.

Step back and take dummy from dog before he drops it.

GUNFIRE

After the pup has learned to fetch the dummy and deliver it to your hand, he must become accustomed to gunfire. For exercise put the dog on a long lead and make him sit. Holding the end of the lead, step away from him. Then throw the dummy as far as you can and, while it is still in the air, fire a training pistol. If the dog breaks, jerk sharply on the lead, repeating the command, "Sit." When he is finally steady, drop the lead and command, "Fetch." Practice this exercise daily, correcting him if necessary, so he learns to remain motionless until you send him to retrieve.

With dog on lead, command "Sit," then throw dummy.

If dog breaks at sound of pistol, pull sharply on lead.

BLIND RETRIEVES

In hunting, particularly from a blind, game often falls out of the dog's line of sight. He must learn, therefore, to find birds he did not actually see. The dog already knows that a series of short whistle blasts means "Come." Now teach him that a single, short blast means "Stop." Once he has mastered this command, have a friend plant the dummy out of the dog's sight. Send the dog straight ahead, then stop him by whistle. His instinct will be to look at you. When he does, call out, "Fetch," and move your arm in the direction of the dummy. If he gets off course, stop him again and repeat the arm signal. As soon as the dog is following your directions, substitute a dead bird for the dummy so he becomes used to feathers and game scent. At this same stage of training, ask a friend to fire a shotgun from about 30 yards away each time you send the dog to retrieve. Have the friend move closer as the dog becomes accustomed to the noise of the gun. Spend about two months on this training.

Dog starts blind retrieve by
moving out on word "Fetch."

Dog stops at whistle, looks
back for your arm signal.

Dog sets out in new direction
as trainer moves arm, body.

Start exercise by holding dog
in sit position at water's edge.

Next, send the dog into water
to retrieve a shackled duck.

When dog returns, step back
and take bird from his mouth.

WATER PRACTICE

Most retrievers are ready to start working in the water after about three months of formal field training. If the weather is very cold, however, it is better to wait a few months longer. The dog will not mind freezing water once he is used to it, but you may frighten him if you start him off with an ice-cold plunge. The best place to begin this training is a shallow pond with a firm, sandy bottom. (Avoid salt water because the dog may try to drink it.) Take the dog to the edge of the pond and, with your hand on his collar, make him sit. Throw the dummy about 10 yards out. Wait until it hits the surface, then command, "Fetch." Most likely the dog will leap instinctively into the water. If he just paddles in, don't be discouraged—he soon will learn to leap. Occasionally a dog refuses to go in at all. If this should happen, have a friend throw the dummy while you stand in the water holding the dog's lead. On the command, "Fetch," pull the dog in and encourage him to swim to you. Once the dog is retrieving the dummy without difficulty, get a live duck and shackle his wings and feet by slipping an old sock with the toe cut out over his body. Then set the duck out about 20 yards from shore (a shackled duck can float well even though it cannot fly) and send the dog to fetch it. When the dog has made a few successful retrieves, set out some decoys so he gets used to swimming through them.

Make a water-shy dog wade in by pulling on the long lead.

WORKING FROM A BLIND

Before the dog is ready to take hunting, he must become familiar with a shooting blind. It is not necessary to have an actual waterfowl blind or even water for this exercise. In fact, many people prefer the convenience of working their dogs in the backyard. Simulate a blind by setting up an enclosure of window screens or packing boxes. Leave a small opening in the front or side big enough for the dog to get in and out. Make him sit inside the blind. Throw the training dummy as far as you can and fire a shotgun in the air, then send the dog to fetch. If he hesitates about leaving the blind, repeat the command. Once he is out, direct him with hand and whistle signals. When he returns, encourage him to leap back into the blind and correct him if he drops the dummy outside. This exercise, besides being vital training for a pup, is also excellent preseason preparation for an experienced dog.

Throw the training dummy from inside an artificial blind.

Fire shotgun and send the dog through opening to retrieve.

Make dog return with dummy through opening in blind.

Sit the dog behind logs to obstruct his view of the water.

WORKING BEHIND OBSTACLES

The next step is to test the dog under difficult conditions. Choose a pond or bay with an overgrown bank that obstructs the view of the water. Make the dog sit behind some logs or deadfalls and take hold of his collar so you can control him. Have a friend fire a shotgun and then throw a shackled bird into the water where the dog cannot see it. Send the dog to fetch it. If he tries to go around the logs rather than over them, pull him back by the collar and give the command again. Follow through with arm and whistle signals to direct him to the bird. He should return over the logs and deliver the bird to your hand. When he has mastered this obstacle training, he is ready to take out hunting.

Send dog over the logs and
into water to make retrieve.

RETRIEVING WILD BIRDS

The climax of your months of training comes when you
take the dog hunting. This is a new and sometimes bewilder-
ing experience for him. It will be easier if you go out alone
at first so he is not distracted by other hunters and dogs. In
the blind the dog should sit beside you motionless while you
shoot. If he seems restless, stroke him occasionally to keep
him quiet. When the first birds are down, your job is over
and the dog's job really begins. It is one he will enjoy, and
if the dog is handled properly, the hunter, too, will derive
deep satisfaction from watching a well-trained retriever return triumphantly with a bird that might otherwise have
been lost.

Dog must be steady in blind
while hunter fires at birds.

Dog should grasp the bird firmly
but gently as he makes retrieve.

THE POINTING DOGS

George Stymiest

A hunter and outdoorsman since boyhood, George Stymiest, 47, first became interested in training pointing dogs while he was with the Police Department of Lambertville, N.J. When, in 1939, he won the National Amateur Field Trial Championship with a pointer named Lebanon Tim, Stymiest decided to leave the police force to work with dogs full time. Since then he has trained close to a thousand bird dogs at his kennels in Lambertville, entered more than 500 field trials and twice won the National Pheasant Shooting Dog Championship.

For control, take dog on
lead to and from the field.

EARLY FIELD PRACTICE

The best time to begin training a pointing dog is when he
is between 8 and 15 months old, after he has learned to respond to his name and to obey simple home commands.
Always take the dog to the field on lead so he understands
you are the boss, and review his basic commands before un-
leashing him. Then let him run free to get him accustomed
to all kinds of terrain. If he is timid about entering heavy
cover, go in first and encourage him by calling him in after
you. Acquaint him with gunfire by shooting a .22-caliber
blank pistol from time to time. When the dog gets out too
far ahead of you, blow a single blast on a training whistle to
make him stop, and then send him off in a new direction by
moving your arm in a sweeping motion. The distance the
dog will range from you when actually hunting is usually

Encourage young dog to enter cover by going in first.

Bring dog back by bending down, calling him by name.

determined by how he is trained now. Decide in advance whether you want a wide-ranging dog (100 to 200 yards) or one who ranges close (40 to 60 yards)—this depends on the kind of hunting you will eventually do—and stop him at approximately the same distance from you each time. In this way the dog will learn the general limits of the area you expect him to cover. When you want the dog to return to you, stop him with the whistle, then stoop down and call him to you by name. Remember to praise him when he reaches you. At this stage of training, it is unimportant whether the dog points or not. Right now you are primarily concerned with teaching him to obey your commands in the field and to gain experience in hunting all kinds of cover. Spend a half hour every day for about two months on this training.

POINTING

When a dog has learned to investigate all kinds of cover and to range within your hunting limits, he is ready to begin pointing birds. In this exercise a single quail can be used over and over again if you tie a short string attached to a piece of wood to its leg. This won't hurt the bird but will prevent it from flying very far. Tuck the quail's head under its wing and plant it in a clump of grass. Put the dog on a 50-foot rope and lead him toward the bird. Remember that he has to face into the wind to get the scent. When he does, he will instinctively go on a natural point. Then talk to him to keep him steady as you move your hands down the rope to his collar. Holding his collar to control him, improve his form by straightening his hindquarters, lifting his forepaw and raising his head. Still talking to the dog, slowly move up ahead of him and flush out the quail with your foot. If the dog remains on point, fire the pistol. If he breaks—and he probably will at first—command "Whoa" and jerk on the rope. Plan on four months of daily training before the dog really learns to hold steady on point.

Tie string and small stick
to bird's leg to limit flying.

Put puppy on a long rope
and lead up to planted bird.

Steady dog with voice and
use hands to improve form.

When dog is on point, move
hands up rope to his collar.

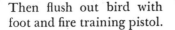

Then flush out bird with foot and fire training pistol.

BEGINNING HUNTING

When you have confidence that the dog will hold a point without breaking, you can proceed to teach him to find a bird in cover and point it without the control and assistance of the rope. A few minutes before taking the dog afield, plant a quail (again use the string and stick for this exercise) under some brush. Release the dog and encourage him with your voice to hunt. If at first he has difficulty locating the bird's scent by himself, direct him to the quail with your arm and body. Wear a bright-colored vest or shirt so the dog can see you easily. When he scents the bird and goes on point, move in to him. Stroke him to steady him and anticipate a break by saying "Whoa." Improve his form if necessary. Then move ahead and flush the bird. When it is in the air, fire the

pistol. Continue to steady the dog with your voice and wait a few minutes after firing to make certain he has held the point. Then reward him, and send him off again to hunt the same quail in whatever direction it may have landed. Spend about two months of half-hour sessions on this stage of training.

Dog will go on instinctive point when he scents bird.

Move slowly up to dog and steady him on point.

Help dog locate bird by signals with arm and body.

If dog holds point, flush bird and fire blank pistol.

ADJUSTMENT TO SHOOTING

Before the dog can go on an actual hunt, he must gain experience at having birds shot over him. Begin this training with planted birds so you know where they are, and use a .410 shotgun until you are sure the dog is accustomed to the noise. Let him hunt on his own, keeping arm signals to a minimum. Talk to him if he runs past the bird or ranges wild. When the dog goes on point, tempt him to break by walking around a few minutes before flushing the bird. This will also teach him to hold the point so that on a real hunt, if he points a distant bird, he will remain steady until you catch up. Continue to talk to the dog as you work up to the bird. Then flush it and shoot. Walk away from the dog slowly, saying "Whoa" if he starts to follow you. Always retrieve your own birds in training. Later, when the dog is experienced and under perfect control, he can be taught to retrieve, although this is not a job he is expected to do. When you bring back the bird, show it to the dog and let him know you are pleased with his performance.

To test dog on point, wait before flushing the bird.

Steady dog by voice as
you flush and shoot quail.

Always retrieve dead bird
in training to show dog.

Dogs honor point of Irish setter
as hunter walks up to flush bird.

HONORING A POINT

After the dog has hunted birds for several months, he is ready to learn to "back," or honor another dog's point. This is the finishing exercise in a bird dog's training. You will need the help of a friend and an experienced dog. Plant a bird and let the older dog point it. Then lead your dog on a rope up to within five feet of him. He may instinctively go on point when he sees the other dog. If he does not, stop him and help him into a point with your hands. When he is steady, have your friend flush and shoot the bird. Keep a grip on the dog's collar and talk to him so he doesn't break. Repeat the exercise on lead until the dog knows what you expect of him; then practice off the lead, encouraging him to back at the sight of the other dog. Eventually he will honor a point from as far away as he can see it. For the bird shooter, there is probably no more thrilling sight in the field than that of one or more dogs frozen motionless as they back another.

3

POPULAR FIELD DOGS

THE FLUSHING SPANIELS

AMERICAN COCKER	ENGLISH COCKER
ENGLISH SPRINGER	WELSH SPRINGER

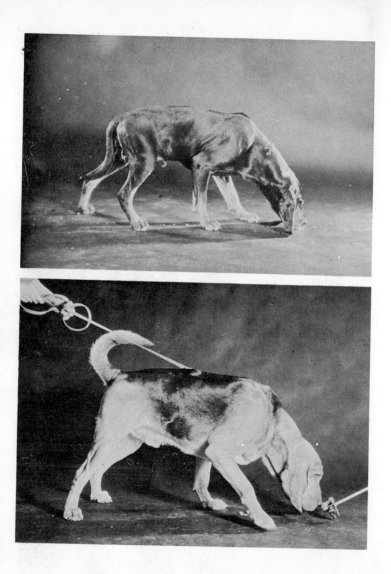

THE TRAILING HOUNDS
BLACK AND TAN COON HOUND
BLOODHOUND

THE TRAILING HOUNDS

BEAGLE

BASSET HOUND

DACHSHUND

THE RUGGED RETRIEVERS

POODLE

IRISH WATER SPANIEL
CURLY-COATED RETRIEVER

THE RUGGED RETRIEVERS

GOLDEN RETRIEVER

CHESAPEAKE BAY RETRIEVER
LABRADOR RETRIEVER

THE POINTING DOGS

POINTER

GERMAN SHORTHAIR

BRITTANY SPANIEL

WEIMARANER

GORDON SETTER

THE POINTING DOGS

ENGLISH SETTER

IRISH SETTER